Enjoy the Holidays

As Compiled by
Old Mountain Press

Old Mountain Press

Published by:
Old Mountain Press, Inc.
PO Box 66
Webster, NC 28788

www.oldmp.com

Copyright © 2020 Old Mountain Press
Copyright © 2020 Individual contributors retain all rights to their included work
Interior text design: Tom Davis
Cover Design: Tom Davis
ISBN: 978-1-884778-45-2

Enjoy the Holidays: A Poetry and Prose Anthology.
Collection: All rights reserved. Except for brief excerpts used in reviews, no portion of this work may be reproduced or published without expressed written permission from the authors or the authors' agent. Included authors retain all rights to their works.

First Edition
Printed and bound in the United States of America by Gasch Printing • www.gaschprinting.com • 301.362.0700
10 9 8 7 6 5 4 3 2 1

Remembering MaXine Carey Harker, an exceptional poet whose work appeared in 30 Old Mountain Press Anthologies. MaXine, we miss you.

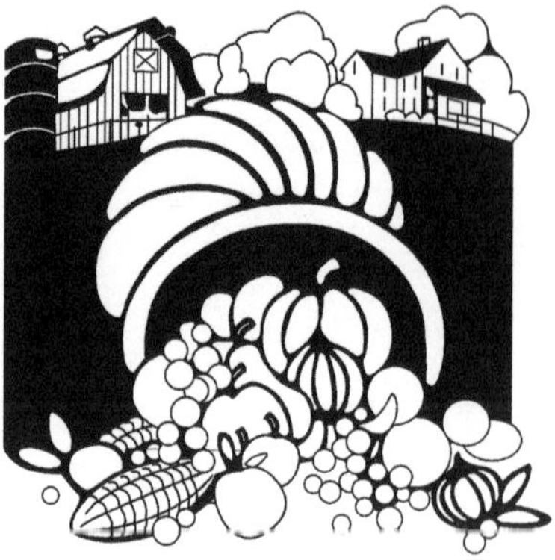

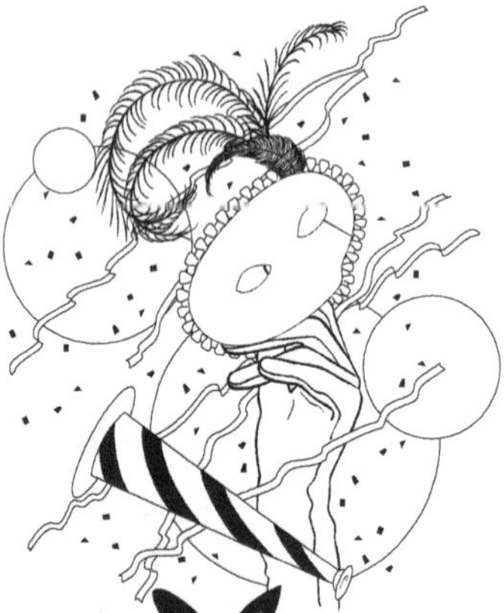

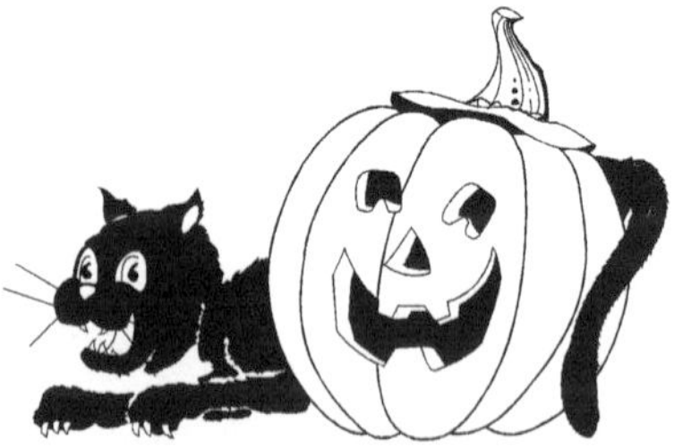

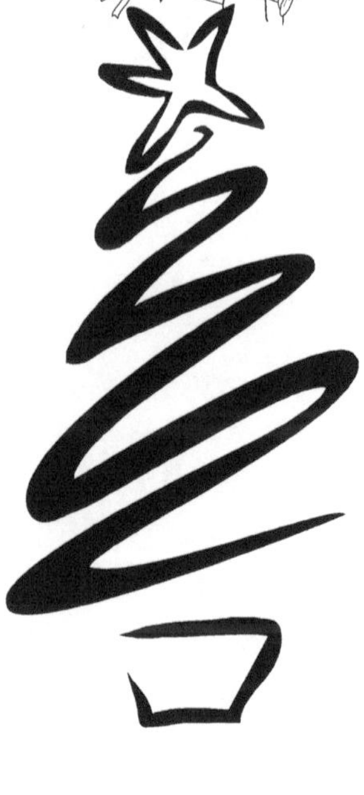

Contents

First Date 1
   Shelby Stephenson
Autumn Captured 2
   Lois Greene Stone
Come, Peace 3
   Nancy Dillingham
Wrappings 4
   Sam Barbee
Snow at Christmas 5
   Glenda C. Beall
Winter's Men (Shakespearean Sonnet) 6
   Lynn Veach Sadler
Winter Sister 7
   Dena M. Ferrari
After I Fed Him Christmas Rib Roast 8
   Michael Gaspeny
Mom's Avocado Refrigerator 9
   Preston Martin
Salutation 10
   Harry Brown
An Old Man Anticipates a New Christmas 11
   Michael Potts
Winter Art 12
   Karen O'Leary
Christmas Presence 13
   Kerri Habben Bosman
Christmas At Gramma Joan's House 14
   Joan Barasovska
January 3, 1947 15
   Martha O'Quinn
Two Views of November 16
   Steve Cushman
Fargo Child 17
   Cindy Larson

Fool's Winter 18
   KD Kennedy
The Spirit of Christmas 19
   Farley Granger
A Child's Memory 20
   Beverly Ohler
Solstice, Specific 21
   Mona Miracle
Quintessential Autumn 22
   Suzanne Delaney
'Tis the Season 23
   Kenneth Chamlee
Autumn 24
   Patsy Kennedy Lain
Christmas Love 25
   Dwight L. Roth
White Friday 26
   Paul Sherman
Cusp of Wonder 27
   Marcia Hawley Barnes
The Christmas Tree 28
   Peggy Dugan French
Stem-dried Raisons 29
   Frederick W. Bassett
Images of Mary 30
   Joanne Kennedy Frazer
Smells Like Fall 31
   Mary Ricketson
Sixteen Reasons
   Why I Will Decorate my House for Christmas 32
   Rebekah Timms
Diminuendo 33
   Jo Koster
At Interval 34
   Glenda Sumner Wilkins
Autumn 35
   Grayson Jones

Molasses-Making 36
   Celia Miles
Oranges in December 37
   Marian Gowan
Stranger's Appearance 38
   Barbara Ledford Wright
Holiday Baking 39
   Blanche L. Ledford
Christmas Cardinal 40
   Brenda Kay Ledford
Auld lang syne 41
   Barbara Tate
Christmas in Paradise 42
   Tom Davis
Christmas in Paradise II 43
   Polly Davis
I'll Be Home for Christmas 44
   James N. Gibson
We May or May Not Meet this Christmas Holiday . . . 45
   Rishan Singh
A LOVEly Tradition 46
   Elaina S. Stone
Goodwill 47
   Elizabeth B. Watson
Cat-o-Lantern 49
   K. A. Lewis
Christmas Dinner with the Reverend 50
   Penny A. Olson

Authors' Biographies 51

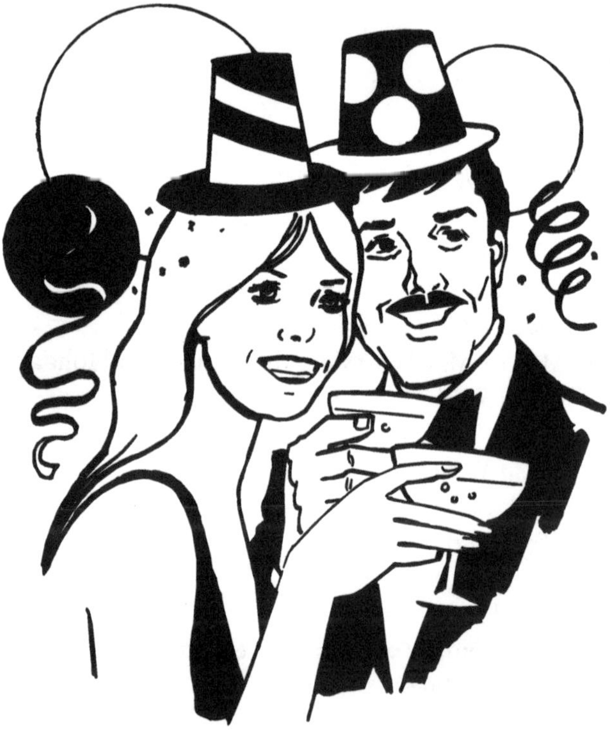

First Date
Shelby Stephenson

My perception is what it is, a raised
Window through falling snow in Buffalo,
A rhyming upper-story where, behold,
Her voice enters my chest as she's yelling,
"I'll be down in a minute," welling
The shout like water dribbling off a dove's
Intractable back, "Do not get too close—
The door—the red's not dry, that door's still wet."
I sit bolt upright in Chip's backseat Saab,
My kind demeanor whirling fuzz in slow
Comfort, hearing my mother pray in low
And steady tones a silent lay she lobs
A thousand miles away from Caroline.
I do not open the door of the small
Auto which seems a far smell from laces
And doilies mother Maytle loves to make.
We hurry—Surrey with Fringes—to eat.
I do not pass Go all night; however,
A stink does spew from Saab's exhaust some bits
Of matter, I recall, the food a treat
For everyone but future revelers
I take inside myself as the real deal.
The vows, I mean; I say we could be trees
Someday lying on ground along rivers
Running water bright and unpolluted
With suds bubbling truth along tangled streams
With little stammering, our lines, givens,
Like choirs filled with words that do not preach,
But praise all gently the score close as bees
At work and play in combs and hives trembling
A squirm as fallen logs flower to teach.

Autumn Captured
Lois Greene Stone

Patch of pumpkins seemed
too large as my son waddled
through orange spheres. His
sweater gathered flakes of fallen
leaves. Propped atop, with tiny
legs dangling, a print-photo was
snapped. Giggling, grandson
ran as if the area were a maze.
He wore the saved cardigan.
A ribbed autumn fruit held this
seated child while a digital picture
was processed. Great-grandson's
tiny sneakers squished moist grass
as he patted pumpkins. Climbing
one, he smiled. My smartphone
clicked, and I instantly
sent images to family.

Published June 2020 *Scarlet Leaf Review*

Come, Peace
Nancy Dillingham

In a world marred
by bitterness and strife
and the apartheid
of loneliness
we long for
the profundity
of wholeness

an increased awareness
of the power
that marches before us

that encroaches upon
and erodes our hard shell
of indifference

leaves us soft
and vulnerable
ready to accept
the white dove

alighting on our shoulder

Wrappings
Sam Barbee

We repeat the graceful thank-you.
What detachment that takes.
Presents for, presents from family
and friends. Wrappings ravaged.

Later, next year's Yuletide paper
waits wadded in the fireplace, bows
collected to regenerate, empty boxes
stacked for the attic.

In recent seasons, gift bags have become
the norm: marketed with seasonal art,
matching tissue paper. Easy to fold
and hide in a drawer. No joyless stairs.

My calendar sags, another holy season
splotched with crossed-out commitments.
At times, preparing for holly-jolly days,
I feel creased and wrinkled, trimmings stale.

Tomorrow, I will sit on the cold hearth:
long for a blaze clear of altered traditions
reasoned as appropriate. Take time to rekindle
Christmas with a pristine approach.

And refuse to recycle the same frills,
festive camouflage for gifts-worth-giving.
Next year . . . wrap with lustrous paper,
joy affirmed with a fresh box and bow.

Snow at Christmas
Glenda C. Beall

Silent December snow covers
grey mountain forests, clings
to thin bare branches of oaks,
poplar and ash.

It mounds on brown wide leaves
still hanging on to stubborn trees
that, until now, denied winter's presence.
Holly bushes crowned with snow

create photo ops for Christmas cards.
Rooftops iced in white,
frosted gingerbread houses,
await Santa's footsteps.

Red ribbons on our mailbox
collect crystal flakes
within curving bows,
on bunched pine boughs.

Kayla hangs her stocking, dreams
of Barbie dolls, gift wrapped boxes
piled high beneath her brilliant
Christmas tree.

We light a candle in the snow.
Pray for children around the world,
who long for peace, a cup of rice,
an end to fear and
war.

Winter's Men (Shakespearean Sonnet)
Lynn Veach Sadler

The winter men seek me because I'm warm,
expecting shield against the dark, dank cold.
Their swarming prophesies the next snowstorm.
The cold concedes foothold on my threshold.

The winter men want simmering hot stews,
hot possets, apple cider laced with rum.
They eat and drink, don't talk
    but watch the news.
So glum, they make the winter but humdrum.

I love crepuscular short days, long nights,
snowflakes a-dance with fairies
    and Snow Queen,
but gloomy wintry men are troglodytes.
The winter's every gift they contravene.

I'll choose a spring or summer man to wed.
At worst, an autumn man will take my bed.

Winter Sister
Dena M. Ferrari

Autumn Maiden to you my Sister one that I adore
I have need of you now to rest as it's my turn to explore
You helped our fevered Summer Sister full of greens and life
Cooled Her brow and softened Her time at the end of Her seasonal life.
Now it is my turn to heal this tight-packed world until
I can cover it in a white blanket
as my blizzard pets bring the chill.

Don't tarry too long my sweet Sister Dear
Life has turned the Wheel of the Year
The North Wind will arrive before it's your seasonal death
So hug me sweet Sister before
You have taken Your last breath
A weary Fall Maiden's soft sigh in the last of Autumns wind
Sleeps in the cold folds of Winter's arms within

The Winter Maiden at last has arrived
Keeps the world within Her frozen lives
Blanket of snow silver blue and white
Winds of the North loosened has taken flight
Howling along it speaks of as it makes the earth colder
Until long last Sister Spring taps Winter's shoulder

After I Fed Him Christmas Rib Roast
Michael Gaspeny

William smiled, toweling goblets squeaky clean
to please me, his mother. Had he ever done
anything wrong—middle-aged altar boy
bearing the crucifix of niceness?
It, too, required a sacrifice.
His wife had taken over his life.

I yelled, *When will you stand up!,*
pounded down the hall, slammed
the bedroom door, turned up *Winter Wonderland*
on easy-listening radio to decibel-hell.
Soon he'd have to ask permission
to eat—her version of saying grace.

Mom's Avocado Refrigerator
Preston Martin

works still, years after. It hums mournfully
against the back wall of the garage, cooling
beer and garden overflow and the birdseed
and suet so mice can't get it.
Long years past Mom cleared the top shelf
to rest the turkey before Thanksgiving.
Her new refrigerator stood in the small kitchen
where someone stirred gravy and someone scooped
green beans to a bowl, or seasoned and fluffed
mashed potatoes one last time. All moving sideways,
tucking arms and elbows *excuse me, move over*,
through the throng, helping manage dinner, carry
to the table before the turkey was prayed and carved.
If Avacado hummed those days we didn't hear
over talk and laughter, the occasional shout or tears,
the toasts of a grown family gathered together,
one more time.

Salutation
Harry Brown

for Sue

A rare and common sight these January mornings,
say at ten or so after twelve or fourteen
the night before, is my small cow herd standing near the top
of the rise behind the barn looking every one southeast,
stock still as if exhumed statues awaiting the Rapture,
the only motion small, thin clouds drifting slowly up
from noses and mouths to quickly disappear in the bright, still
    quiet,
and steam slowly rising from frosted backs to dissolve
in the icy air while this motley congregation, half their bodies
spread in obeisance before old Helios,
                                warms.

I leave these winsome oblations
for private matins
before my kitchen Yotul.*

*Norwegian wood stove

First published in *The Chautauqua Journal* (2016).

An Old Man Anticipates a New Christmas
Michael Potts

Time to savor a season, holiday (holy-day),
aunts and uncles arriving, wood on a winter's
fire, gifts under a needled cedar, walnuts
over wood, a nutcracker's crunch, carols
on vinyl, 33 rpm, and on TV, Rudolph,
Frosty, the Grinch, the Little Drummer Boy,
Amahl and the Night Visitors—childhood
memories fly by, their smoky trails thinning
with age, routine, and loss—parents,
grandparents, aunts, uncles passed beyond
this world into (The Hope) a perfect one.

The Hope is made flesh, a baby, born
on a straw bed, horse and donkey
witnessing, Joseph watching, relieved
to be under shelter for his young wife
and new child. Shepherds leave sheep
to visit the Author of Hope, Preserver
of Stories in his neverending mind,
fading thoughts living again in vivid
reality with no fear that they will disappear
from an aging brain. Let me be a child
again, in bed waiting, knowing that this
Christmas shall be more than memory.

Winter Art
Karen O'Leary

White
crystal
winter gems
elegantly
cling to barren trees
dressing imperfections
in a long shimmering gown.
Art that twinkles in the moonlight,
beckoning nature's viewers to pause
and share in the splendor before it melts.

Christmas Presence
Kerri Habben Bosman

Silent Night.
My hands
chop, chop, chop,

Holy Night.
slice, slice, slice,

All is calm.
wrap, wrap, wrap,

All is bright.
scrub, scrub, scrub,

Round yon virgin Mother and Child.
mix, mix, mix,

Holy Infant, so tender and mild.
love, love, love.

My hands feel my mother and grandmother,
the years of chopping, slicing, wrapping,
scrubbing, mixing,
loving.

Sleep in heavenly peace.

Christmas At Gramma Joan's House
Joan Barasovska

High on a hill in North Carolina,
up a steep road in a green wooden house,
Gramma Joan waits and waits for Christmas,
waits for a family from way down South.

A tall, tall tree stands in the living room,
eight feet high and covered with lights.
From its green branches hang hundreds of ornaments,
birds and fuzzy animals, stars and balls red and bright.

Ryan knows there's a basket of toys to play with:
blocks, trucks, and a musical Ferris wheel,
a Jack-in-the-box, puppets, Raggedy Ann and Andy,
and a giant Teddy bear waiting for a giant Ryan hug.

Gramma Joan's got a recipe to bake with Ryan,
gingerbread men and gingerbread boys.
She has a stool for him to sit high on
to decorate cookies for Santa's big night.

In the living room there's a pile of Christmas books:
Rudolph, The Snowman, The Grinch, and more!
Gramma plans to read them all to Ryan,
sitting side-by-side in her cozy red chair.

Here's what Santa will see when everyone is sleeping,
when he tiptoes in the quiet house on Christmas Eve:
gingerbread men and a note from Ryan
and lights all a-twinkle on the tall, tall tree.

January 3, 1947
    Martha O'Quinn

Mama's soft touch awakens me.
I peek from mile-high blankets and quilts
protecting us from January.
Sleet pelts the tin roof; little sister stirs beside me.

I struggle to focus on Mama's words.
We're going to the hospital for our new baby.
I remind her, *baby brother!*
It may be a sister. You'll love her, right?

I can't hurt her feelings. *Yes*
She turns to leave, I think **it must be a brother!**
I burrow back into warmth and sleep;
an aunt is there to care for us.

You have a brother, says the aunt.
Sister and I plan names for him.
Arriving home, he already has a name.
We plan his life instead.

Two Views of November
Steve Cushman

It's November again and Julie stands
at the back door, shakes her head, says,
I hate fall, something she says every year,
all those leaves, so much mess to clean up.
I don't tell her how much I love this time
of year, cool nights, return of sweat pants
and sweat shirts, the cold another excuse to
hug her and all those beautiful leaves raining
down on us, but instead I walk up behind
Julie, hug her tight, say *I know, my love, I know.*

Fargo Child
Cindy Larson

Relentless wind of the Great Plains,
howling, moaning through window frames.
Bedroom walls painted ice blue.
Slipping into a troubled sleep.

Little red boots climbing street-plowed,
dirt-blackened, road-ridges.
Yearning for fresh snow-cover
to soften the somber mood.

Fuzzy earmuffs, mittens-on-a-string.
Frosty face-scarf firmly knotted in the back.
Words snatched at their birth...
unheard...wrested by ruthless wind.

Intervening years sweeten the memory,
now from a grayer point of view.
This old oak tree twice transplanted,
finally savoring Southern sun.

Fool's Winter
KD Kennedy

When the humidity of Summer flees
and touches the cool of Autumn nights
we mix seasons in a confusing way.
A lap of warmness chased by a streak of
cold wind when birds are confused and
fly south, then north, not knowing
Summer from Fall.
Pretty dry and windy and fine feeling,
we can date the days fleeing ahead of change...
...we have Indian Summer all over us.
Full fledge Fall fights like fury to be free.
Then it is and Indian Summer passes
like those original Indians died on the
plains of the old west.
Autumn has its wing-ding mildness for a
few months and around Christmas a
cold wave hits hard. The start of Fool's
Winter is upon us.
For a week and then Winter happens
with a few reversals to reasonable
weather, then cold, then warm, then
solid cold again.
Fool's Winter will give you The Cold, The
Flu, Covid virus, and assorted other
sickness treats.
Fool's Winter is messy, unpredictable,
wet, and scary to name a few traits.
Bear with him.
It can mess up all its sibling celebrations
of Halloween, Thanksgiving, Christmas,
and New Years. And it does!
Fool's Winter, Indian Summer, Sprinkly
Spring, and Late Winter were all
designed to mess us up ! And Do!
This is weather change, not climate change.

The Spirit of Christmas
Farley Granger

My Truth I Sold for Bread.
My spirit vanished for greed.
Christmas was vapors alone.
Love simply I would not heed.

My lady was rare and mighty.
Her soul much too good for me.
Her care for the smallest in life
Was compassion for others to see.

She fell upon the poorest of health.
I would not help with her life.
Our children condemned me, alas,
For not giving care to my wife.

One night I fell upon sweats.
A dream of her death hammered me.
I awoke in a daze, stunned and drawn,
Seeing how I'd come to be.

I fell prostrate on the floor.
Remorse ravaged my soul.
The spirit of Christmas returned
With majesty joyful and bold.

I bought back my truth with love.
My spirit returned as it should.
Christmas was there with great glory.
My lady came back well and good.

A Child's Memory
Beverly Ohler

Were you naughty or nice?

Nice we affirmed,

though truth be known

there was a mixture!

Never the less

the toys piled high

under the tree.

Forgiven

Loved

MERRY CHRISTMAS!

Solstice, Specific
Mona Miracle

Joy warms my ears
as I recall a precocious speck
which eased its self-embrace,
unleashed a cosmic sneeze,
so suns could fire a tilting dance of spheres
and let some parts grow elegant landscapes
where now my carbon atoms and such
enliven consciousness in me
that home lies on this globe's north half,
where snowy solstice bursts with scents
of cinnamon and pine
and shining chimes for ears and eyes.
This confluence of carbon and such—
effects of chance or grace—
awaken me with awareness
of change beyond a long night's end
that celebrates another light:
the solstice gift inside a heart.

Quintessential Autumn
Suzanne Delaney

Autumn's story is full of rustic shades
that echo deep from every vale and hill
Of splendour and of forest colonnades
as one by one they float and spin and spill
in frosted shadows and in evening's chill

Dogwoods change in carmine escapades
to celebrate old summer's standing still
Scarlet leaves and tints of Marmalade's
Shiraz, Clarets, and Burgundies distill,
bright tones of nature for the soul to swill.

Amber, Apricot and Goldenrod brigades
capturing our gaze and hearts to thrill
Piles of forest treasures spilling in cascades
with dappled browns and Caramel's goodwill,
all opulence of Autumn to fulfill.

'Tis the Season
Kenneth Chamlee

Folded to the pillow, my pulsing ear
crunches like a lumberjack in snow.
A drunken man with holly palms
and skate-blade knees
crawls around in my brain. He burps
and sets a candle in each eyesill.

Ache wraps my throat in its tight scarf,
grips the shoulders like a heavy pack,
twisting down my back and legs
as fever tumbles me in kaleidoscopic dreams.
Stretching, then curling,
I sweat through deserts and tundra.

Downstairs, the children come in singing
"You'd better watch out" and shed
their glistening coats in a wet flop.
I hear them rush the tipsy tree, shake
and count the packages, then
herded like recalcitrant reindeer

they ascend, transformed now into
cherub magi bearing gifts of pills,
thermometer, and soup. They pat my hand
and encourage me, invite me
down from my spinning reverie
to wait with them in wonder.

Autumn
Patsy Kennedy Lain

Summer shifts, raging
fall colors boldly burst
warn winter follows
as wooded dense branches
of reds rustle, turn faded blue gray,
let go, drop patterned cascades
of multi-hued lacy leaves
to scatter, fly, land
underneath for stomping
walkers, sneaky grove dwellers
to crackle, crumble purple
into golden amber, ginger
and lemon tones atop
speckled burnt sienna
grasses turned rusty brown
after that last cut.

Feral forest critters squirrel away
caches, create stashes
of crushed, crunchy berries, fruits,
seeds along with nuts
before cold sets,
some creatures
make ready to hibernate,
nuzzle up in knot holes,
root into underground burrows
as wicked winds whisper cooler air,
naked towering trees rattle, shake
bushes, shoot swirling pine needles
through the air like piercing darts;
curly crooked twigged
arms stand dreary
leaving bare bleakness.

Christmas Love
Dwight L. Roth

Unpacking Christmas a box of loving gifts
Full of sweet memories that bring me a lift
Remembering my students' love shared with me
Ornaments of beauty to hang on my tree
A shiny brass apple with name and date
A stained glass window made on a plate
Homemade Rudolph made with clothes pins
Cotton ball snowman and angels with wings
So many memories from yesteryear
Much love remembered sweet and clear

Grandchildren come to help each year
Oohing and awwing is what I hear
And I smile remembering back on those days
When love was shown in so many ways
My tree's not filled with bought decorations
But a tree filled with love from a past generation
And when it's all over we'll pack them away
Storing the love for another Christmas day
I treasure the gratitude each one brings today
Feeling the love that will never goes away

White Friday
Paul Sherman

Snow falls, huge flakes in rush
to cover up. Two Santas
unload from El Camino
as teller counts cash. I glance past
cleavage of depleted savings,
feel a blast of cold hit.
Fit Santa does the splits, busts
knee on tile, flings pistol, clattering,
to the launderer giving two-weeks
notice to the vexed lead.

Fat Santa withdraws when toy's
lifted with plastic laughter,
risk analyst rises from behind desk.
Trio of execs charge like stags leaping
toy heaps to be first rack on St. Nick.
Fat Santa fends initial fury,
manages brief chokehold on the lead
with his own, grinch-faced tie,
before capitulating to the pungent
aroma of cheap American cologne.

The teller keeps composure.
Asks if I seek closure.
I pull tiny metal cap gun from pocket,
point to the heart-shaped locket
on her chest,
request a stack of Benjamins.
She fires a look of disgust,
slams cash drawer shut.
Franklin, she flares, *I'm not your slut.*

Cusp of Wonder
Marcia Hawley Barnes

silence fills the room
interrupted only by slips
of tissue falling

a short full Fraser fir
dressed in tiny clear
glass lights blinks

my daughter watches
until the tree is filled
and steps away

the cat comes near
curiously touching new
straw beneath three kings

old fingers rest
baby Jesus in a manager
silence fills the room

The Christmas Tree
Peggy Dugan French

It shines
   inviting us to gather
      and celebrate.

The close of another year
   is right around the corner
we gather with friends
   and family
      sometimes all alone
just to celebrate the love that is here.

It sits there
beautiful
   pure
inviting us to stop
for a short while and reflect
and take stock of the good things
   that are ours
forget about the homework for a minute
   the dirty dishes
      unwrapped presents
and just savor the holiday warmth.

It brings us together
   adorned with familiar ornaments
   and twinkling lights
      that spark memories of years past
for a few off-key Christmas carols
   a glass of wine
      and a toast to a new year ahead
   with all things possible
with new beginnings
   and a fresh start
      ours for embracing.

Stem-dried Raisons
Frederick W. Bassett

For years my boyhood Christmas gifts
included a box of stem-dried raisons.
Then for some reason unknown to me,
they were just a fond memory.

On hearing that story, my mother-in-law
persistently shopped until she found a box.
There they were just for me
my first Christmas morning in her house.

Over the years, Vinnie Lee Roberts
endeared herself to me in many ways,
but for that act alone, I forgave her
for trying to talk Peg out of marrying me.

Images of Mary
Joanne Kennedy Frazer

Christmas card Mary…
   serenely seated, veiled
   in blue and white gazing
   at her arm-cradled infant
   enclosed in a celestially-lit crèche
   angels singing on high

No room in the inn Mary…
   teenage Jewess Miriam
   giving birth on a bed of straw
   mid-wifed by Yoysef surrounded
   by scents and sounds of animals
   in whose home she lay

Flight to Egypt Mary…
   fleeing from Herod
   who would harm their child,
   she seeks refuge in a foreign land
   with betrothed and babe.

Archetypal Mary…
   representing refugees
   compelled yet today,
   to run from terror
   into unknown futures

Published June 2019 in Being Kin Chapbook

Smells Like Fall
    Mary Ricketson

One layer of mist, high on the mountain top,
unabashed by the waking world below

takes its time, thins its veil till fabric weakens,
green mountains show, and blue takes over.

Down on the ground, air smells like fall,
staghorn sumac already wears its autumn hue.

Purple stalks of Venus looking glass flower
by goldenrod and lavender thistle

next to a worn out field of corn,
one ear left to pick, besieged by weeds.

Virgins bower, her blooming mass of white,
covers faded unknown clumps of leaves and saplings.

Last of the queen Anne's lace still stands innocent
on the side of the road for all to see.

Red stalks of cardinal flower stand full bloom
in the middle of a slow stream where no one looks.

Mostly I don't care who knows this beauty,
just so I can watch the rose of Sharon open for the day.

**Sixteen Reasons
Why I Will Decorate my House for Christmas**
Rebekah Timms

When leaves begin to fall the Christmas spirit within
me churns up a chink-chink-chink of sleigh bells ringing

Never mind that coronavirus has callously dictated my
empty December calendar....I stare blankly at closet
shelves filled with treasured Christmas decorations

And I feel like a little girl whose favorite doll
is missing and she is too sad to look for it

The list of decorating ideas created last January with
the hope of delighting my guests this Christmas lies
tauntingly on top of my favorite invitees address book

The theme of my living room tree was to be *music*
when I expected to fill my house with various groups of
friends and family to celebrate the Christmas season

Yesterday while imbibing a couple of glasses of wine
I polished sixteen decorative brass horns of various
sizes and styles, trumpet, bugle, coronet, French
and as I cleaned the Brasso from my fingernails, face
and kitchen countertops, I vowed to decorate my house
as usual

My guest with whom to share the splendor of the
music-themed tree and my customary twelve other trees
will be my new mischievous orange tabby kitten
Princess Taffy who'll no doubt challenge my impulsive
decision to polish those brass horns

Diminuendo
Jo Koster

She used to go through
six boxes of Christmas cards a year
loving handwritten notes
inserted photos
family newsletters

Now just a handful sit on her desk
amidst a mound
of loss and absence

It used to take her weeks
to make all the cookies and treats
cheerful holiday clutter
of dragées and chopped nuts
tins of fruitcake
soaked weekly with rum
welter of ribbons and foil
and warmed spice aromas

Now she can do it all in a day
So few boxes to pack
So few houses to visit
So few faces to delight

Finding the joy takes work now
why iron the linens
or deck the halls

And yet she dons her apron
picks up her pen
and paces the old familiar steps

Telling herself the dance itself
not the result
is what counts

At Interval
Glenda Sumner Wilkins

I trace the creek
with my eyes
wondering where
the river runs
winding past the chapel
as autumn approaches
trailing over cobblestones
and village benches.

The orange brilliance
of turncoat leaves
transforms an uncertainty
of mid-life
into a current
I can understand

Now. . . I'll wander
where the river runs.

Autumn
    Grayson Jones

A premonition in the wind
heralds the season, ushers in
this time of change, taut with tension
between keen joy and apprehension
at the signs of coming days:
the cries of geese through evening haze,
morning fog, a sharper chill,
dry rustle of grasses, standing still
with asters grown in bright profusion,
tangled, blown in wild confusion.
Autumn dresses with a flair!
Wagers all. Holds nothing spare.
Clean air crisp. A sky too blue.
Trees ablaze in shattering hue.
Still, Autumn yields her share of sorrow.
Impassioned beauty fades tomorrow.
Somber tones; cold, grey rain
give expression to the pain.
Branches sigh; leaves are scattered
as if their brightness never mattered.
Autumn dares not weigh the cost
of risking all... for all is lost.

Molasses-Making
Celia Miles

KEATS' "ODE TO AUTUMN" paints the season as one of stillness, a drowsy easeful, winding-down time. But my uncle's fall activity—molasses making—was anything but calm. Children buzzed around competing with the bees, being swatted away from the work at hand. A day of strenuous work strewn with gossip and male jollity, molasses-making seemed the masculine counterpart of women's quilting bees.

Girls tended to stay back from the sticky, messy job. The boys were put to pulling in the stalks of cut cane and bringing wood for the fire going under a large metal boat-like vat. My uncle patiently, then wearily, fed the stalks into the "press," careful not to "stop it up" or slow it down.

My eyes followed the poor old horse as, attached to a long pole, it plodded round and round. Sometimes we patted the animal or offered an apple. The cane was pressed, and a stream of juice flowed from the press and ended up over the fire. There men or boys constantly skimmed off the gray-greenish suds from the boiling liquid with ladles or poles with pieces of tin hammered onto them. As the sun blazed down, we girls eyed the boys, giggled, slapped at the bees buzzing around or nursed their stings. Overcome by the heat or steam, plenty of bees plummeted into the frothy stew.

The logistics of the operation are lost in my memory. In went the stalks of cane, out came juice directed into a flat bottomed pan, wide and flat, with slanted sides. The "cooked off" cooled liquid became sorghum molasses, put in jars and jugs, providing sweetening through the year.

Molasses making was a day of sweat, stickiness, sunshine, sweetness, bone-weariness, repetitiveness. It was part of making a living the best way you could. It was nothing like poetry—even in memory.

Oranges in December
Marian Gowan

DO YOU BELIEVE in Santa Claus? Like so many things in life, it's complicated. As early as four years old, I understood that Santa had help. On Christmas morning, when I saw the large cradle under the tree, I knew that it had been made by Mort Hoffman, a deacon in my father's church. And a few years later, I knew that the Ginny Doll wardrobe had been carefully crafted by my mother. Even though she was mindful always to close the master-bedroom door when she was sewing, I knew she was making doll clothes. The Featherweight sewing machine would run a few seconds, then stop, then start, then stop. Had to be short seams, not like when she was making my school clothes.

So why is my belief complicated? I knew that the red felt stockings my older brother and I had were a gift from our Aunt Mona. Mine had a white cuff on which I carefully had written my name in pencil in capital letters (the only kind I had learned to write). Adorning the front were felt cutouts of toys, with sequins. A yellow truck with red wheels, a pink Jack-in-the-box, a black and white drum, a candy cane, a ball, sequined all.

Even though Santa had help with the larger gifts, I knew that he, alone, filled the stockings. Who else would know I wanted silly putty, or a new Pez dispenser, or the special dark chocolate bar? And the most special treat of all, the large orange in the stocking's toe? Imagine oranges in December! Only Santa could do that.

Until I discovered the bag of oranges in the refrigerator.

Stranger's Appearance
Barbara Ledford Wright

A BLAST OF WIND howled, and I pulled my coat tighter. I jerked open the door to my classroom at Gardner-Webb University in Boiling Springs, NC. This was my last class for teacher renewal credit. Now I looked forward to the Christmas season granting me some peace of mind.

The professor met the students and urged us to hurry and take our test because a snow storm had reached Cleveland County, NC and would soon be in Boiling Springs. We were a noisy bunch when we left, scrapping chairs, and tromping feet to gaze upon a world draped in a blanket of white.

I was the last one to reach my car in the parking lot. I'd guessed that all the other people had long distances to drive. I only lived in Shelby and took my time to enjoy the snowflakes sifting softly from pewter colored clouds. I slammed against my door. I panicked and jerked the handle. It wouldn't budge. Where was my cell phone? What would happen to me? Would I freeze to death? I prayed that someone would find me.

Truth be told, I expected the worst outcome. But a shimmer of hope came as light broke through the darkness. An old beat up truck sputtered its way beside my car. A long-legged man loped over to me. I wasn't afraid because he looked like "Jackie" Robinson—the first black American baseball player in the major leagues. He lit a match to the key slot and the door opened. I blinked my eyes in disbelief.

The stranger told me to be safe. He didn't leave until I had started my car and edged through the parking lot. The last thing I saw of him was an arm held high and a hand waving. He called out, "Be safe Miss, and Merry Christmas!"

Holiday Baking
Blanche L. Ledford

MAMA TRESE LEE started her holiday baking a week before Christmas. The aroma of apples, spices, oranges, and a black walnut cake baking in the woodstove filled her kitchen.

Brother George, my sister Oma, and I gathered walnuts in the Trout Cove. We sat on the front porch and hammered the walnuts. It took a lot work to get a cup of kernels, but we savored Mama's delicious black walnut cake that she baked each Christmas.

I enjoyed helping Mama bake in her kitchen. She let me lick icing from the bowl and taught me the tricks of culinary art. None of the modern baking shows on TV today could compete with her expertise.

She was also an expert at making jelly. She didn't use Sure Jell like modern folks. Mama actually made preserves from apple peelings. Cookies, cakes, pies and thumbprints filled with grape jam graced her table at Christmas.

Even as an adult, I spent a lot of time at the kitchen table talking about life with Mama. She sipped black coffee, nodded her head, and listened. Her blue eyes sparkled and with a smiled she asked me to sample her treasured desserts. I could always count on Mama to give me her full attention and to bake delicious goodies for Christmas.

Christmas Cardinal
Brenda Kay Ledford

BOB LEDFORD CAUGHT a train to LaVeta, Colorado in 1915. He worked as a cowboy on a ranch and relished breaking broncos.

He fulfilled the quest for adventure, but longed for home in the Blue Ridge Mountains. Bob also missed his sweetheart, Miss Minnie Matheson. Her beautiful face appeared every night in dreams.

One day he grabbed his gear and headed to the Matheson Cove. When Minnie saw Bob, she ran and threw her arms around him. He proposed and she said, "You old goosey thing!' They got married at Myers Chapel and lived in a two story white-washed house on Long Bullet Creek.

Minnie's baby was born a year later. Doc Killian delivered Rondy at home. Life was almost perfect for the young couple. Bob worked the farm and Minnie doted on her boy. She looked forward to another child.

But tragedy struck. World War I raged and a global pandemic killed 20 million people. Minnie got the Spanish flu and Robbie Lee died shortly after birth.

When Christmas arrived, Minnie loathed the festivity. She refused to attend the play at church. A cardinal landed on her kitchen windowsill. It lifted cheerful songs and gazed at Minnie. She felt like it was a message from baby Robbie to live again. Christmas filled her heart with peace.

Auld lang syne
Barbara Tate
...and then there were four

THE PHOTO FROZE five around a table for six, an Oklahoma Choctaw, three Texans and a dark haired Italian from Ohio, dressed in their last laundered clothes, toasting Le Havre and the women they'd meet, toasting Galveston and the women they'd left.

"The Marine's have landed gents, yessiree, the Merchant Marines have arrived. Merry Christmas!"

They toasted themselves for a safe Atlantic crossing on an oil tanker that had zigzagged through a minefield of enemy subs, sang every carol they knew, had a waitress take photos and celebrated Christmas which they never thought they'd see.

The Italian from Ohio ordered another round, saluted and announced he was going to pledge allegiance to the French Foreign Legion. They blew foam into clouds and quaffed mugs to the would-be deserter who had already deserted in his mind. He'd crossed the line and couldn't get back, a drifting outsider adrift in the unknown.

Near dawn the Choctaw and three Texans toasted their final toast to their drifting friend and stumbled back to their ship, arms entwined singing what they could remember about old acquaintances that should be forgot.

"What'll we tell the Captain?"

"Tell him war is hell. Then we'll tell him the truth."

"And what's that exactly?"

"Damned if I know. Rubino never was one to pull pranks."

"What'll we tell his mom when we get back to the States? I heard if you sign up you're never heard from again."

"Maybe he'll turn up. I bet he's back at the ship asleep in his bunk. Well hell, he doesn't even know French."

"Yeah. But you never know. War changes a guy. Do you really think they'd let him sign up?"

"Who knows. We're probably worrying over nothing."

Seeds of sunrise tinted the eastern sky as they climbed the gangplank....and the photo froze five and then there were four.

Christmas in Paradise
Tom Davis

For our honeymoon, Polly and I spent a "wonderful" weekend in Panama City, Florida. Money being the big factor. But we vowed to do better at some point in our future. Better would be our second Christmas together in Hawaii.

We had talked about it for several months, and when I got a free ticket and a reduced rate on hers, that sealed the deal. We were leaving for a five day stay in Honolulu!

I always hated flying, especially long flights. Polly and I, both tall, always found airplane seats cramped. Sitting in the rear of the aircraft with my knees up around my ears, the stewardess took pity and said that there was an open seat in first class if one of us would like it. I turned to my traveling companion, pulled out a quarter, flipped it, and lost.

The flight finally landed, and it took me forever to muscle my way from the back of the plane to the door. There waited Polly, all smiles, rested, jumping up and down, and waving like she hadn't seen me for six months. Easy for her to do.

We checked into our hotel room 16 floors up with a view of Waikiki beach. We bought matching blue shirts dotted with little white palms trees, and for the next five days, we lay in the sand, drank colored liquids laced with rum from odd shaped glasses, and, of course, got tickets for the Don Ho show and heard him sing "Tiny Bubbles." On Christmas day, we rented a car and drove around the island stopping for lunch at a little hamburger joint. Money still being a factor.

But all good things must end, and we sat in the airport waiting for her flight back to the states. The call came, and we walked to the boarding check in, tickets in hand. I was antsy to say the least. Polly was trying not to cry. Me, too. I gave her a hug and a goodby kiss and watched her turn and walk toward the plane, glancing back from time to time. My flight back to Vietnam wouldn't leave for another three hours. *Oh well*, I thought. *Look on the bright side. I'll see her again when my tour is up in six more months.* Or so I hoped.

Christmas in Paradise II
Polly Davis

I WENT TO graduate school and he went to war. When I received a letter saying we were cleared to spend Christmas during his R&R in Hawaii, I was ecstatic. My suitemate's husband was also in Vietnam, but after eight months, she had heard nothing of R&R. I felt guilty.

The day finally came. All I remember from the flight was the packed, cramped plane and the women, mostly wives, heading for R&R.

As we exited the plane, Hawaiian women, clad in grass skirts, placed a lei of fresh exotic flowers around our necks. That was when reality set in, setting my nerves on fire. I was really going to see the man I married, as yet untouched by the horrors of Vietnam. We'd been married just a year before he left for the War. I checked into the hotel on the beach.

Early the next morning the bus picked us up in staggered intervals at the hotels where we wives were staying and took us to the airport where we had landed the day before. By then we were communicating with each other. As the planes came in, the men deplaned one by one, taking forever, it seemed. They all looked alike in their khaki uniforms, so we began moving forward little by little to better see their faces. Several men had already found their wives, locked bodies, and moved off behind the plane for privacy.

Fewer and fewer seemed to be exiting. A chaplain came to tell a waiting wife that her husband would not be coming. This took the line of remaining wives by surprise until the reality set in. I choked back a tear. Finally, I thought I saw Tom coming down the airplane steps. We rushed into each other's arms; then we backed off and stared.

We managed, though, to find each other in the confusion, to see the island of Oahu in a rented car, to attend a Don Ho show, and to attend a genuine Hawaiian luau. Then it was time to send him off again. Not an easy thing when you're sending your love back to war. But he would be returning home in another six months, *if* we were lucky.

I'll Be Home for Christmas
James N. Gibson

MY WORK TOOK my wife and me to Michigan, far away from the farming community where I grew up in West Tennessee. But Mom and Dad always had a Christmas dinner waiting when our extended family gathered for the holidays. During the early years, my wife, our young son, and I traveled by car from Michigan, later Virginia and then Minnesota, setting out in winter cold, driving for many hours, arriving late if bad weather didn't delay us for the night. Somehow we always made it to the old, white two-story house on the hill and gathered with our siblings, extended family and friends for our yearly celebration of the reason for the season.

Years passed, and I accepted a job in Taiwan, Republic of China, nearly 8,000 air miles from West Tennessee. My wife made a home for us in an apartment in Tien Mu, a suburb of Taipei.

As director of the Human Resources department of an automobile manufacturing complex, I faced a difficult wage and benefits negotiation with the employees' Union the second year I was there. A strike could shut us down and cause serious financial harm, so there would be no "break" for Christmas. I let the family know, and then focused my full attention on the challenges at hand. Somehow Santa found us at our apartment. My wife and I opened our gifts from home, and our gifts to each other on Saturday, Christmas morning. That night we celebrated quietly with another couple over dinner at a local restaurant. I realized that our traditions are what make us Americans; cultural norms make us who we are. I didn't miss them until I couldn't be home to share them.

As I stood on the balcony looking out over the night lights of Taipei, the lyrics of a song came, unbidden, to mind: "I'll be home for Christmas, if only in my dreams."

We May or May Not Meet this Christmas Holiday
Rishan Singh

I THINK IF YOU and how we spent Christmas last year. I wish we could relive our dreams, and everything we wanted to do in our free time. We took ourselves away from each other, because we know we'll be able to make it on our own. The last few years have been full of blasphemy and melancholy. I always knew that we can't stand by each other, but you kept me in the dark, and you never abused me. My life changed for the better, but it was so sudden that before i knew it, everything vanished. I wish i could end it, end it and move on, but the year we ate together I'll never forget. I made a mistake in 2012, and it costed me.

The pot roast, the pastries, the cream pies, are very dear to us. I'm sure you remember how we played "truth and dare" around the Christmas table, and you could tell when I was happy, numb and sad. There was a lot going through my mind, but the lock down of mid-June 2020 ruined everything. It was like Christmas passed early this year, and I could tell something was missing in my life. I'll always love you and miss you, even I can't reveal who you are this Christmas.

The cherished memories of Christmas always remain with me. You vanished away from the shards of glass that create a mirror of other people knowing me. I feel misfortunate, lost, and I will wait for you, like always.

A LOVEly Tradition
Elaina S. Stone

VALENTINE'S DAY WAS anticipated in elementary school. As February chills hung in the air, we knew hearts, chocolates, and happiness were just around the corner.

After Christmas and New Year's break, there weren't many decorations dotting the hallways. Soon, though, the classrooms would be showing strings of red-and-pink ribbons, fabrics, and twisted crepe paper.

I knew an important competition was coming up. A letter box where our special valentines, and, more importantly, where THE candy would eventually be held, was to begin. The person with the most glamorous box would win a special prize. The routine swung into effect.

Step 1: find an old shoebox somewhere in your house.
Step 2: buy glitter, paint, and stickers to make your box stand out among your friends.
Step 3: find the coolest Valentine's theme-card set that the supermarket offers.
Step 4: grab your student roster and write some cheesy line on each Valentine.
Step 5: save the best candy (fun dip) for your best friends or your crush.

When the day came, everyone would wait and get ready to swap Valentines and stick them in each other's overly-decorated shoeboxes. The competition would ensue, and giggles would fill the room.

The next best part of February 14th was going home and showing my parents the candy and Valentines I received. Did I get one from a cute boy? What did my best friend say? The excitement lingered on as well as the sugar from all the sweets.

The tradition and happiness it brought made me want to share this fun activity with my students as a teacher now.

Goodwill
Elizabeth B. Watson

TRAVELING FROM SOUTH Florida and South Carolina, four lively grandchildren and their parents added exuberance to our Christmas celebration. We were fortunate to live in the NC Blue Ridge Mountains at 3000'. On the 26th we woke to a cloudless *Carolina blue sky* and a wide view of pristine, glistening snow. The excitement easily equaled that of Christmas morning.

Eager to go out, but unprepared for the weather conditions, we scrambled to clothe the clan in heavy outerwear. Although the offerings for the children were oversized, no one fussed. A blessing, they came with thick-soled athletic shoes.

Spontaneous laughter accompanied the bundled-up crew as they raced out to trample down the white lawn spread. The snow was perfect to sculpture, wet and sticky. Guided by experienced adults, a unique character emerged. A fat carrot became a nose and food container lids made startling black eyes. Grand-Pop, a former pipe smoker, added an essential prop, a remnant of his old habit. We stuck the pipe in the mouth, a circle slice of red pepper. Our figure was no longer gender neutral.

I found a colorful tartan scarf and a knit cap for the cold head, plus large gloves worn for shoveling in past New England winters. We tucked the thumbs of the handwarmers over a bright orange extension cord, which defined the waist. Finally, snow hiking poles, adorned with red bows, were stuck into the snow on either side. Pleased with our cool master piece, we posed for candid shots until a snowball fight commenced.

Often winter conditions at lower elevations were apt to be cold rain and black ice, not white precipitation. Consequently, as roads dried, traffic increased significantly on our quiet street. Our lawn became the perfect setting for photos. We made instant friends with a delightful family from Alabama, whose children had never met a live snowman. As they clustered around our jolly guy, whom we dubbed **Goodwill**, I swear I saw smugness in those big black eyes.

Holiday Traditions
Carol Passmore

WHEN I THINK of holiday traditions, I think more of changes than traditions. The first time I cooked Christmas dinner for the family, there were a few complaints. Yes, the cornbread stuffing was good, but we always have bread stuffing. As for the raw cranberry relish, only my father and I thought grated horseradish root was an acceptable addition.

But there have been so many changes. When I was six we lived in small town Tennessee and drove out to an empty field to saw down a cedar. Who knew milk came from cows and Christmas trees grew in fields.

In a small town in the mountains of eastern Kentucky, we learned how fortunate we were, which didn't mean that I could understand why I didn't get a horse for Christmas.

Back in NC I was 14, my sister 11 and my brother 7 when guess what, a baby brother and Christmas with a little kid again. I left for college and came home one Christmas the eldest of five. My sister had a friend whose mother died and whose father was unable to care for her so she moved in and eventually my parents adopted her. I must confess to a bit of annoyance before I moved to "the more the merrier" theory of life.

I married a man with similar holiday traditions. We moved to Colorado, had our first child, and continued to go home for the holiday. But Colorado weather is a bit changeable and as we drove from Boulder to the Denver airport we went from sunshine to blizzard condition and all flights were cancelled. We were lucky enough to get an airport motel room Our two year old amused himself running from window to window shouting "Boats, Mommy, Boats." We did make it for Christmas Eve and declared further visits would happen in the summer.

We had two more children and generally stayed at home, celebrating with whichever of my siblings were around. One year my brother showed up with a girl, who despite her introduction to the family, decided to marry him. Now there are grandchildren and everyone is scattered. I am sure the corona virus will change many holiday traditions, at least for this year.

Cat-o-Lantern
K. A. Lewis

HALLOWEEN FELL ON Saturday that year, and after lunch it was carving time. I'd bought a huge pumpkin, tall instead of wide. I set it down on newspapers, cut a 'lid' in the top and laid it aside. Then I scooped out the goop and scraped the interior clean with a big metal spoon. I drew a wickedly grinning cat face onto the pumpkin with magic marker, then cut out triangular ears, setting them upright with toothpicks in front of the holes, so they were lit from behind. Now an inverted triangle nose. Then the wide crescent mouth, with fangs and a split upper lip. And the eyes, the most difficult. Large and moon-round with spindle-shaped pupils. Lastly, I poked holes between upper lip and nose, and above the eyes, and added lots of whiskers, white pipe cleaners, kinked and curled. I set tealights inside and cut a cleft in the lid for smoke.

And it was ready, my Cat-o-Lantern.

I put Cat-o-Lantern on the front step and lit the candles. Lots of families came trick or treating that night, and I got many compliments. But the big payoff came just after dark. A young mother carried her little girl to my door, wearing the cutest homemade costume I'd ever seen—a faux-fur lion outfit with a thick yarn mane, dangling tail, and feline face make-up. She set the toddler down and I put candy in her bag. Then the tiny lion turned and saw Cat-o-Lantern. They were nearly the same size. She roared in delight, "Mommy, mommy! Look!" More children were arriving, and her mother called for her. On to the next house. The toddler followed Mommy, then ran back. She hugged Cat-o-Lantern and grinned, two cat faces glowing together. As her mother led her away, the little lion girl stared over her shoulder at Cat-o-Lantern, until she disappeared into the Halloween night. My favorite Halloween memory.

Christmas Dinner with the Reverend
Penny A. Olson

As the Christmas tree twinkled, all colors of light and presents lay open under the tree. Two sisters sat in their chairs, starring into the fire.

Three days had passed since the dreadful news about Reverend and Mrs. Walsh. Rumor had it they were found in their home, headless on Christmas Day. The sheriff had come to the sister's house the day after Christmas asking questions about Christmas Eve and the guest Tom Leonard.

"The Reverend and Mrs. Walsh told us about Mr. Leonard and asked if we would mind if they invited him to Christmas Eve dinner. We said, please, bring him, didn't we sister?" Sister said to the Sheriff.

"He was charming, and he ate plenty. It was nice to see a young man eat so well. Sister and I commented on how well he ate. They stayed after dinner, had a few drinks, said Merry Christmas, and left around 10:00 pm. It was a lovely evening." The other sister said smiling sweetly.

"Mr. Tom Leonard is a serial murder. He chooses the clergy as his victims. Easy prey. You two are lucky you still have your heads. Got any coffee?" asked the Sherriff.

The Sherriff thought it might have happened Christmas Day. Speculation only, as he was waiting for the coroner's report. Sipping his coffee, he told the sisters there had been three previous murders: all the same way, all to clergy on past Christmas Eves, all in the general area. The sisters listened as they sipped their tea.

The sheriff laid his cup on the table. "Merry Christmas, ladies. Let me know if you think of anything I should know." And he left.

"Well, who will we invite next year for Christmas Eve dinner, sister?"

"I imagine the new Reverend. Someone will have to replace Reverend Walsh."

"Tom will want another head or two for Christmas, Sister."

"Yes, he will, Sister, yes, he will."

Authors' Biographies

B

JOAN BARASOVSKA lives in Chapel Hill, NC. Joan is an academic therapist in private practice, working with children with learning disabilities and psychological challenges. She cohosts a poetry series at Flyleaf Books and serves on the Board of the North Carolina Poetry Society. Joan has poems published or forthcoming in *Kakalak*, *San Pedro River Review*, *Madness Muse Press*, *Red Fez*, and *Main Street Rag*. *Birthing Age* (Finishing Line Press) is her first book of poetry.

SAM BARBEE poems appeared *Poetry South*, *The NC Literary Review*, *Crucible*, *Asheville Poetry Review*, *Main Street Rag*, *The Southern Poetry Anthology VII: North Carolina*; plus on-line journals *Vox Poetica*, *Courtland Review*, and *New Verse News*. His second poetry collection, *That Rain We Needed* (2016, Press 53), was a nominee for the Roanoke-Chowan Award as one of North Carolina's best poetry collections of 2016; and is a Pushcart nominee.

MARCIA HAWLEY BARNES is a Georgia writer and poet. Publishing credits include "Popcorn Overlook" published in 2020, Old Mountain Press. The author has written three children's books and is a free-lance writer for the Clay County Progress. Barnes lives in Towns County, GA.

FREDERICK W. BASSETT is a retired academic who turned to creative writing late in life. His poems have been widely published in journals and anthologies. He also has five books of poetry. His revised and expanded edition of *The Old Stoic Faces the Mirror: A Life in Poems* was published in November, 2019. He has two published novels—*South Wind Rising* and *Honey from a Lion*—and is editing the third novel of this trilogy—*The Winter is Past*. Widowed, Bassett currently live in Greenwood, SC, near his son Jonathan and family.

GLENDA C. BEALL lives in Hayesville, NC where she works as program coordinator for NCWN-West. Her publications include a family history book, *Tom Council and his Descendants*, *Paws, Claws, Hooves, Feathers and Fins*, a collection of short stores and poems, *Now*

Might as Well be Then, a poetry chapbook, published by Finishing Line Press. Her poetry has been published in numerous literary magazines, online and in slick publications for over twenty years.

KERRI HABBEN BOSMAN is a writer in Chapel Hill, NC. She is a graduate of Peace College and North Carolina State University. Her work has been included in the *News and Observer* and regularly appears in publications throughout the United States and Canada. After allowing it to linger, she is returning to her manuscript of personal essays and poetry.

HARRY BROWN holds degrees in English from Davidson College, Appalachian State University, and Ohio University; and taught English at Eastern Kentucky University for some forty-three years. Harry has published six poetry collections, and co-edited an anthology of Kentucky writing. His two latest collections are *Felt Along the Blood: New and Selected Poems* and *In Some Households the King Is Soul* (Wind Publications). He lives with his wife Alice in Burlington, NC.

C

KENNETH CHAMLEE (Mills River, NC) is Professor Emeritus of English at Brevard College in North Carolina. His poems have appeared in *The North Carolina Literary Review*, *Cold Mountain Review*, *Ekphrasis*, and many others. He won ByLine Magazine's National Poetry Chapbook Competition (*Absolute Faith*), and the Longleaf Press Poetry Chapbook Competition (*Logic of the Lost*). His poems have appeared in six editions of *Kakalak: An Anthology of Carolina Poets*. Learn more at www.kennethchamlee.com.

STEVE CUSHMAN has published three novels and the poetry collection, *How Birds Fly*. He lives with his family in Greensboro, NC.

D

POLLY DAVIS, ED.D, is retired from the NC Community College System where she served as an English department chair and an administrator. She served as a trustee for the Cumberland County Library and Information Center. She is the editor of *Daddy Pa's Diary*, and *Growing Up Southern in Baconton Georgia*. She has written and published her memoir: *Stumbling toward Enlightenment*. She is an avid reader and supporter of the arts in North Carolina. Polly lives in Webster, NC.

TOM DAVIS' publishing credits include *Poets Forum, The Carolina Runner, Triathlon Today, Georgia Athlete, The Fayetteville Observer's Saturday Extra, A Loving Voice Vol. I* and *II, Special Warfare.*, and Winston-Salem Writers' POETRY IN PLAIN SIGHT program for May 2013 (poetry month). He's authored several books. Tom has recently completed his memoir, *The Most Fun I ever Had With My Clothes On A March from Private to Colonel.* He lives in Webster, NC.

SUZANNE DELANEY is a Retired RN who now enjoys creating Mixed Media, writing and taking inspiration from Nature. Her work has been published in several Old Mountain Press Anthologies and her current book, "Poems of Nature Enchantment and Mystery is available on Amazon. Born in Australia she now enjoys living in Asheville, NC.

NANCY DILLINGHAM is associate editor of the on-line poetry journal *Speckled Trout Review.* Her latest work is *Like Headlines: New and Selected Poems* and the chapbook *Revelation.* Her collection of poems *Home* was nominated for a 2010 Southeastern Independent Booksellers Alliance award (SIBA). She lives in Asheville, NC.

F

DENA M. FERRARI is a regular contributor to OMP, Dena's poetry are featured in Westchester Community College of NY *Phoenix* (1975), Writers Alliance Poets World-Wide anthologies has many of her published works. Dena's own books, *Poems From the Hearth* (2010) *Come Closer My Dearies* (2013), *Charmed Times Three* (2015), and her newest book *Wyld Earth Magick* (2018) shows diversified writing styles, leaving a Living Legacy for her grandchildren. She and her husband, Peter live in Vass, NC.

JOANNE KENNEDY FRAZER is a retired peace and justice director and educator for faith-based organizations. Her work has appeared in over 25 anthologies, on-line zines and magazines, most recently in *New Verse News.* Five poems have been turned into a song cycle, titled *Resistance*, by composer Steven Luksan, and performed in Seattle and Durham. Her chapbook *Being Kin* (CreationRising) was published in June 2019. She lives in Durham, NC.

PEGGY DUGAN FRENCH is a California girl with Minnesota roots. She has been the editor of the small print zine Shemom since 1997. Her work has appeared in Lilliput, bear creek haiku, Shemom and Whispers. She has worn many hats over the years, but raising her children has been one of her greatest pleasures. Peggy lives in Cardiff, CA, with her husband, cat and wild garden and blogs at www.peggyduganfrench.com

G

MICHAEL GASPENY'S third chapbook, *The Tyranny of Questions*, a novella in verse, is available now from Unicorn Press. His previous works are *Re-Write Men* and *Vocation*. He has won the Randall Jarrell Poetry Competition and the O. Henry Festival Fiction Contest. Living in Greensboro, NC, he has received the Governor's Award for Volunteer Excellence in recognition of his hospice service.

JAMES GIBSON, Northville, Michigan, featured Native American culture in the five novels in his "Anasazi Quest" series. His eighth novel, *To Live or Die in Taiwan* was published in 2018. He is presently working on a sequel, *To Live or Die in Panama*. Review all his books at www.PentacleSPresS.com. *Anasazi Princess* and *Anasazi Journey* are now available in Kindle format on Amazon.com.

MARIAN GOWAN is author of *Notes from the Trunk*, published by Old Mountain Press. Her work has appeared in many Old Mountain Press anthologies and southern regional publications. She retired to the NC mountains from western NY in 2001, but in 2017, returned to western NY to be near family. (mariangowan1@bellsouth.net)

FARLEY GRANGER thinks more than he writes, and he writes more than he sees other people. He grew up in a depressed country town and understands the struggles of poor, heartland folks. But he has a lot of hope. Farley lives in La Grange, NC.

J

GRAYSON JONES lives in Young Harris, GA, and teaches biology at Young Harris College there in the north Georgia mountains. Her poems have appeared in *Appalachian Heritage*, *Corn Creek Review*, *Poetry South*, *Slant* and *The Healing Muse* and in anthologies by Old Mountain Press.

K

K. D. KENNEDY, JR. has published Eight Books (8) books of poetry, short stories, and essays: *Our Place On Time, Waiting Out In The Yard, For Rhyme Or Reason, Progenitors: A Kennedy Genealogy, The Works Of K. D. Kennedy, Jr., Poems Worth Remembering, Family...Forever's Lovesong,* and *Truth Instead.* He has also published works in over forty anthologies and periodicals.

JO KOSTER and her cat Max live in Rock Hill, where she teaches at Winthrop University and waits for the pandemic to end. A new collection of her poems is forthcoming in summer 2021.

L

PATSY KENNEDY LAIN continues to reside in Hubert, North Carolina. She writes and paints mostly inspired by her imagination, surroundings and life's quirkiness. Patsy's works have appeared in local papers several magazines and many anthologies over the years. She has won multiple awards and honors for her works through her local senior center.

CINDY LARSON, a native of Fargo, North Dakota, lived with her husband, Jerry, in southeastern Connecticut for 33 years. They built their retirement home on Glassy Mountain, Landrum, South Carolina, and it was their favorite location for 17 years. Currently they are residents of The Woodlands, a senior living facility on the edge of beautiful Furman University, Greenville, SC.

BLANCHE L. LEDFORD is a native of Clay County, NC. Her work has appeared in many Old Mountain Press anthologies and journals. She writes about her Southern Appalachian heritage and received the Paul Green Multimedia Award for her book, *Planting by the Signs.*

BRENDA KAY LEDFORD is a native of Clay County, NC. Her work has appeared in 43 Old Mountain Press anthologies. She won two gold medals for her essay and short story in the Clay/Cherokee Senior Games Silver Arts Literary Contest for 2020. She's an award-winning writer and published in many journals.

K. A. LEWIS graduated from the Corcoran School of Art in 1986 with little idea of how to make a living. Her work experience includes cake decoration, jewelry sales, hypnosis certification, being robbed at gunpoint, and 32 years as a custom picture framer. Since 2014, her poetry and genre fiction have been published in several anthologies. Katy and her husband live with five demanding cats in a small book-stuffed house in Falls Church, VA.

M

PRESTON MARTIN has published poems, or has forthcoming, in *New Ohio Review, Iodine, Tar River Poetry, Chaffin Journal, Kakalak, Snapdragon, Appalachian Heritage, Pine Mountain Sand* and *Gravel*, and other journals and anthologies. He lives in Chapel Hill, NC.

CELIA HOOPER MILES is a native of Jackson County and now lives and writes from Asheville. A retired community college instructor, she has recently published her tenth novel, the third in a series of "cozy and clean" mysteries all set in western NC: *The Skeleton at the Old Painted Mill: A Marcy Dehanne Gist Mill Mystery*. www.celiamiles.com

MONA MIRACLE, born in a Kentucky mountain valley, has lived in California, Michigan, Florida; and for thirty years, Asheville, N.C. Mona was a featured presenter at South Florida Poetry Society, and a four-category winner in Florida Freelance Writers Annual Competition. Readers can sample her publications, including the novel *Wesley's Gift* at Monaraemiracle.com; Amazon provides her ebooks and print formats. Currently developing a non-fiction book, she is researching technology and attitudes for successful aging.

O

BEV OHLER has been involved in theater, art and creative writing all of her life, much of it working and teaching at Warren Wilson College. Her early life in the Northeast appears in many of her books, and published material, although she loves living in NC. She contributes regularly to OMP, and lives in Black Mountain.

KAREN O'LEARY is a writer and editor from West Fargo, ND. She has published poetry, short stories, and articles in a variety of venues including, *Frogpond, Setu, A Hundred Gourds, bear creek haiku, Shemom, Creative Inspirations* and *NeverEnding Story*. Karen feels blessed to be a part of many Old Mountain Press Anthologies. She edited an international online journal called *Whispers:* http://whispersinthewind333.blogspot.com/ for 5 ½ years. She enjoys sharing the gift of words.

PENNY OLSON loves to write. She currently lives in Weaverville NC with her wonderful husband Scott of 49 years and three rambunctious dogs. Her heart is divided between Weaverville and Tampa, Florida where her son and his lovely family live. She is blessed by many wonderful nurturing friends

MARTHA O'QUINN'S work has appeared in 39 previous OMP anthologies. She and her husband lived in WNC for 22 years and in 2018 moved to Georgia to be near family and former friends. Her poetry and non-fiction reflect her southern heritage, born in NC and living in four other southern states. Martha has four grandchildren and five great-grandchildren, all subject to starring in poetry or prose.

P

CAROL PASSMORE attended UNC-G, married and had three children, all born in Boulder, CO. In 1980 the family moved to Durham, NC where Carol worked at the reference desk at the Durham County Library. Since retirement she enjoys reading, gardening, yoga and writing poetry. She contributed to and co-edited a book of Quaker children stories which was translated into Russian.

MICHAEL POTTS authored the novels, *End of Summer, Unpardonable Sin* and *Obedience* as well as the poetry anthologies *From Field to Thicket* and *Hiding from the Reaper.* He lives with his wife, Karen, and ten cats in Coats, North Carolina.

R

MARY RICKETSON lives in the Appalachian Mountains and works as a mental health counselor. Her poems often reflect the healing power of nature, surrounding mountains as midwife for her words. Her recent published collections are *Hanging Dog Creek, Shade and Shelter,* and *Mississippi: The Story of Luke and Marian.*

DWIGHT ROTH is a retired elementary school teacher of 29 years, who grew up in the mountains of Southwestern Pennsylvania. He enjoys writing poetry, painting, and music. He had his work in several OMP anthologies. He has self-published four memoirs and four books of poetry and three children's books. He has nine books or booklets on Amazon Kindle. He and his wife Ruth live near Monroe, NC. He writes daily on his blog: https://rothpoetry.wordpress.com

§

DR. LYNN VEACH SADLER, writer/editor, lives in Burlington, NC. A former college president, she has 5 books and 72 articles and has edited 23 books/proceedings and 3 national journals and published 3 newspaper columns. Her creative writings are 11 poetry chapbooks and 4 full-length collections, 125+ short stories, 4 novels, a novella, 3 short story collections, 2 nonfiction collections, and 2 volumes of plays (another in press). She was Central Region Gilbert-Chappell Distinguished Poet 2013-2015.

PAUL SHERMAN lives on the side of Mt. Mitchell outside of Burnsville, NC. His poems have appeared in several anthologies of Old Mountain Press as well as *Silver Blade*, and *On the Inside of Outhouse Walls*. He would like to wish a Merry Christmas to each and every writer who ever attended the WA Writers Retreat.

RISHAN SINGH has been instrumental in recognizing and promoting upcoming talent in South Africa, with events such as the World Scholars Cup being initiated at the Playhouse Theater. Through a record of outputs, he has attained commercial success, as well as, critical acclaim. He was recognized by the eThekwini Municipality in 2014, and the Golden International Honor Society in 2006. Apart from being published in the sciences, he is immensely involved in the arts. He can be contacted at rshnsingh@webmail.co.za.

SHELBY STEPHENSON is the author of *Family Matters: Homage to July, the Slave Girl*, Bellday Books, winner of Bellday Prize. His most recent book is *More*. He lives near Benson, North Carolina, where he was born and raised.

ELAINA SARAH STONE'S publishing history includes poetry in Shemom, The Jewish Press, and Mountain Places. Her professional works, involving children with Autism and literacy needs, have been published in *Building Blocks* magazine. Ms. Stone is a second-year, 5th grade, special education teacher. She lives in Pittsford, NY.

LOIS GREENE STONE, writer and poet, has been syndicated worldwide. Poetry and personal essays have been included in hard & softcover book anthologies. Collections of her personal items/photos/memorabilia are in major museums including twelve different divisions of The Smithsonian. The Smithsonian selected her photo to represent all teens from the 1940's-50's. She has been nominated for Best of the Net, and twice for Pushcart Prize.

T

BARBARA TATE is an award winning artist and writer. Past President of the Tri-County Society of Fine arts in Cuyahoga Falls, OH she is a member of the British Haiku Society, the Haiku Society of America and Haiku Canada. Her work as been published in *Storyteller, Santa Fe Literary Review, Modern Haiku, Contemporary Haibun Online* and *Akitsu Quarterly*, as well as dozens of anthologies. She has a son, Duane Booth, 3 grandchildren, Justin, Brandon & Kaitlin, and great granddaughter Aubrianna in Akron, OH. "Even at my age, I'm still a work in progress".

REBEKAH TIMMS lives in Greenwood, SC with her cat. She has four sons, seven grandchildren and three great-granddaughters. She has published a memoir of her mother and a collection of poems. She is currently working on a collection of poems, prose and short stories. Rebekah enjoys writing and feels that her work is an expression of her gratitude and joy of life.

W

ELIZABETH WATSON, in these trying times of the pandemic, finds writing her stories like soul food for her. It nourishes her as does the happy memories of that Christmas when the Watsons shared the joy of creating **Goodwill**. (Like a snowman's melt down, may this virus disappear soon.) She and her husband look forward to celebrating in person with family and friends in Greenville SC and horizons beyond. Recently, she tallied up 22 of her short works published in Old Mountain Press and is pleased to have longer pieces accepted in other anthologies as well.

GLENDA S. WILKINS grew up on a North Carolina tobacco farm, and believed she'd never live beyond the county line. Decades later, she moved with her husband to Europe for a dozen years. Her poems have been published in Europe, Great Britain, & North America.

Thus far, she appreciates several poetry awards. She lives on an air strip, Winterville, NC.

BARBARA LEDFORD WRIGHT'S inspiration to write stories about her life and ancestors comes through many hours of family history research. Her work has appeared in many online entries, journals and anthologies, and almost all of the Old Mountain Press Anthologies series. Barbara resides in Shelby, NC.